MENTORING THE *NEXT* GENERATION

A Strategy for Connecting the Generations

Mel Walker

REGULAR BAPTIST PRESS
1300 North Meacham Road
Schaumburg, Illinois 60173-4806

MENTORING THE NEXT GENERATION:
A STRATEGY FOR CONNECTING THE GENERATIONS
© 2003
Regular Baptist Press • Schaumburg, Illinois
1-800-727-4440
www.regularbaptistspress.org • www.rbpstudentministries.org
Printed in U.S.A.
All rights reserved
RBP5294 • ISBN: 0-87227-998-7

Contents

108800

Dedication

This book is dedicated to two men who mentored me in ministry:

Pastor Roger Mills, my senior pastor when I began my ministry as a youth pastor; and

Dr. Gordon Shipp, my "boss" when I started my college teaching ministry.

Both of these men are in Glory now, so they will never know how much I appreciate the impact they had in my life and how much they taught me. I know their heavenly reward will be great.

Preface

REMEMBER WHEN you were a kid? Did someone make a significant impact on your life? You know the person I'm talking about—the adult in your church or school who took the time to encourage you. He may have been a coach or band teacher. Or she may have been a youth worker or Sunday School teacher. He may have been the parent of a friend, your pastor, or youth pastor. Or she may have been another caring adult who took the time to notice you and support you in the things of the Lord. Many of us were fortunate enough to have an adult who took the time to encourage us by the little things he or she did with us and for us.

Back then we didn't have a name for these people, but today we call them "mentors." *They are the trusted adults who take the initiative to develop growing, personal relationships with students and encourage their spiritual and personal maturity.* These mentors are adults who care enough to notice and to support the teenagers in their churches.

As I look back on my days as a teenager, I fondly remember the caring, godly encouragement of older people in my church. They were not necessarily the "official" church youth workers, although those people greatly influenced my life too. I am talking about the adults who took the time to say an encouraging word to me, send me notes, or call me on the phone. (Yes, we had phones back then!) I still remember those adults who prayed with me when I was struggling with something or who came to my high school basketball games. Some provided spiritual encouragement; others encouraged me just by taking an interest in my activities and my walk with the Lord.

We live in a busy world. Yet I believe that many adults could have a ministry in the lives of the teenagers in their churches. They just don't know what they can do. These people may not have a lot of time, but they are willing do what they can to encourage students. Perhaps mentoring is a trend whose time has come in youth ministry. Today's students need all the encouragement they can get.

Timothy Smith quoted this statement, which was based on a 2000 Gallup survey, in his book titled *The Seven Cries of Today's Teens:* "We live in a society [where], despite widespread concerns about children and teenagers, the vast majority of adults are not actively involved in the lives of young people outside of their families. . . . Without the attentions of many adults in all parts of their lives and community, young people are deprived of important sources of guidance, nurture, care, and socialization."[1]

There is a simple but effective way for adults to interact with and encourage teenagers: It's called mentoring. This book, *Mentoring the Next Generation,* contains simple suggestions for the adults in our churches who would like to be involved in some way in the lives of teenagers.

CHAPTER   1

The Biblical Basis of Mentoring

In the last few years the concept of mentoring has come into vogue in many business and educational settings. Experts are writing books and hosting seminars to describe and teach the basic concept of mentoring. (For an example of what is available today, take a look at these secular Web sites on the subject: www.mentoring.org and www.whomentoredyou.org. A selected bibliography is also included in the back of this book.)

The word "mentor" supposedly originated in Greek mythology. In Homer's *The Odyssey*, "Mentor" was the character entrusted with tutoring Odysseus' son and providing guidance and instruction in the absence of his father.[2] "Mentor" illustrates the concept of mentoring.

I define mentoring as *a caring adult who takes the initiative to develop a personal, growing relationship with an individual student to encourage spiritual and personal maturity.*

develop a personal, growing relationship with an individual student.

The impetus is on the adult's showing the student that he or she truly cares and wants to be involved tangibly in the young person's life. The adult initiates the relationship because he or she understands that the student needs instruction and guidance.

Many of us were the recipients of that kind of attention when we were kids. Most likely, our lives are lined with caring people who took the time to be personally involved with us. Do you remember the impact of caring adults in your life? It is probably the little things those adults did you for that you remember the most. In the same way, mentoring is not necessarily a commitment of a huge amount of time on the part of the adult. Quite the contrary, mentoring often involves little things, such as showing someone attention and encouraging his or her walk with the Lord.

The Harvard Mentoring Project challenges us with these words: "Growing up, were there people in your life who encouraged you, showed you the ropes, and helped you become the person you are today? Think about family members, a teacher or coach, a neighbor, a boss, or family friend; those people were mentors to you. Most successful people say they had mentors along the way who guided and encouraged them. . . . General Colin Powell points to the influence of his father; Senator John McCain credits a high school teacher and coach whose example helped strengthen his resolve during years of imprisonment in North Vietnam; and Oprah Winfrey cites a fourth-grade teacher, Mrs. Duncan, who taught her to believe in herself."[3]

Mentoring often involves little things.

Undoubtedly those mentors made a profound influence in the lives of their students or protégés. This book, *Mentoring the Next Generation,* focuses on the spiritual impact that caring, godly adults can have on the lives of the impressionable students in our churches.

God's Word contains real-life illustrations of spiritual mentoring relationships. To get a glimpse of the Biblical basis for this kind of ministry, let's take a look at some key New Testament passages.

1 THESSALONIANS 2:7–12

We discover Biblical principles that form the basis for mentoring in passages such as 1 Thessalonians 2:7–12. Note verse 8: "So being affectionately desirous of you, we were willing to have imparted unto you, not the gospel of God only, but also our own souls, because ye were dear unto us."

The apostle Paul shared the gospel and his life with the Thessalonian believers. These two priorities form the foundation of a mentoring relationship. Effective mentors take time to teach God's Word to students. In addition, they share their lives with students. Paul indicated that he was "affectionately desirous" of the Thessalonian people. This wording demonstrates a constant yearning for an intimate and personal relationship. We can translate the phrase "we were willing" as "delighted," or "thrilled." Paul "delighted" to share these things with the Thessalonians.

Communicate the truth of God's Word.

Let me expand on these two basic priorities for a healthy mentoring relationship. First of all, a spiritual relationship begins with a commitment to communicate the truth of God's Word. Notice the emphasis that Paul placed upon "the gospel" in 1 Thessalonians 2 (see verses 2, 4, 8, and 9). Spiritual mentoring is not just developing a personal relationship between a caring adult and a maturing student. The mentor bases that relationship upon the precepts of God's Word. Paul did that during his ministry with the Thessalonian believers. He also emphasized this priority in the account of his ministry in Thessalonica, recorded in Acts 17:1–15. Note, for example, verse 2: "And Paul, as his manner was, went in unto them, and three Sabbath days reasoned with them out of the scriptures."

The second basic mentoring priority is a desire on the part of the mentor to share his or her life with the student. The word Paul used for "souls" is the common word for "lives." We discover in the book of Acts that the apostle did not spend a significant amount of time in the city of Thessalonica; however, when he was there, he demonstrated his love by sharing his life with the Thessalonian people. Mentoring is not easy; it takes a commitment of time and effort. First Thessalonians 2:9 supports that thought. "Remember, brethren, our labour and travail: . . . labouring night and day."

In verses 7 and 11 of 1 Thessalonians 2, Paul used a family metaphor to identify the two key characteristics of an effective mentoring relationship: (1) a loving mother ("nurse") and (2) a hardworking father. The Biblical language in verse 7 illustrates the gentle love of a nursing mother. Probably nothing could be as special as that kind of human relationship. There is something very warm and tender about a mother's love for her children.

Have you ever watched a Sunday afternoon professional football game where a hulking defensive lineman has just made an incredible play in the mud and sweat? The camera zooms in on his dirty, toothless smile, and with a cheesy wave, the first words out of his mouth are, "Hi, Mom."

Yes, there is something special about a mother's love. Just as mothers are absolutely indispensable to the growth and development of children, spiritual mentors are essential for the spiritual maturity of their students.

Paul's second illustration in this text is a hard working father. Mentoring takes time and hard work, and it certainly takes adults who love students. The fact that my father worked hard and diligently is my most vivid memory of growing up with Dad. Even now in his retirement years, he is not the kind of guy who can sit around with nothing to do; he still works hard. His dad, my grandfather, was just the same. I remember his strong work ethic. At age sixty-five my grandfather faced a mandatory retirement from his work, so he got another full-time job that he held for more than twenty years—until he died in his late eighties.

Mentoring takes adults who love students.

By using the analogy of a hardworking father, Paul demonstrated that mentoring is indeed hard work. The wording in 1 Thessalonians 2 stresses that a father's role includes modeling and motivating. Notice verse 11 of our text: "We exhorted and comforted and charged every one of you, as a father doth his children." Effective mentors enjoy this kind of ministry with their students. The next verse explains the goal of this extreme effort: to "walk worthy of God, who hath called you" (v. 12). Paul's goal for the Thessalonian believers must be ours for our protégés. Obviously, we want them to grow up to live godly lives. The fulfillment of that goal requires gentle love and hard work, but isn't that exactly what we want for our students as well? Mentoring can encourage the fulfillment of that goal.

TITUS 2:1–8

We find another Biblical example of mentoring in what I call the "Titus 2 Principle." Notice the intergenerational emphasis in this passage. Older women are instructed to teach younger women; likewise, older men are to minister to younger men.

It is a shame that the modern church has gotten away from connecting the generations. I am afraid that we are making a terrible mistake in our church youth ministries if we totally separate the teenagers from other age groups. I have visited church after church where the teenagers have very little to do with  the adults and the adults very little (if anything) to do with the teens. Don't get me wrong. I am a firm believer in youth ministry. I fully understand that culturally and socially teenagers need and want to be around other teenagers. It's just that our kids also need the influence of godly adults. I also believe that adults need the influence of youth.

Developing intentional mentoring relationships in

our churches can help restore the adult-to-youth connection. As well-known Christian educator Howard Hendricks has written, "Whatever you do, get different generations involved with each other, rather than segregated from each other, as is often the practice."[4]

The Scriptures contain multiple illustrations of intentional intergenerational connections (for example, Moses and Joshua, Elijah and Elisha, and Paul with Timothy, John Mark, and others). Yet even a quick look at history reveals that our contemporary culture has done more to separate the various age groups than any at other time. Since the cultural advent of adolescence and a youth culture, we have separated and disconnected the generations in our schools, churches, and other social institutions. Our culture divides children, youth, and adults into separate age groups that have very little to do with the other age groups.

The Titus 2 Principle teaches us that this age group division is not the standard for the church. In fact, I believe that it is natural for older people to want mentoring relationships with younger people. Titus 2 encourages older people to mentor younger people in the following general categories: the teaching of Biblical truth and the development of character qualities, people skills, family relationships, and outreach.

Titus 2 encourages older people to mentor younger people.

Paul taught that older men and older women are to

teach and model godliness in order to encourage the younger men and women in specific areas. The word "teach" in verse 4 could be translated "to train," or even "to encourage." Kenneth S. Wuest puts it this way: "to make sane or sober-minded, to recall a person to his senses."[5]

These intergenerational relationships are essential. Older women can and should train and encourage younger women; likewise, older men can train and encourage younger men. The church is supposed to work this way. Instead, our churches normally divide people by age groups; therefore, the youth and adults have very little to do with each other.

Intergenerational relationships are essential.

Adult mentors should be identified in our churches as those who have the ability to fulfill these instructional responsibilities in the lives of the upcoming generations. This concept will work if we give it a chance.

BARNABAS

Scripture gives a vivid illustration of one man who had mentoring relationships with almost everyone who came into his life. Those around him nicknamed him "the encourager," or "the son of encouragement." By now you know that I am talking about Barnabas. His real name was Joses, or Joseph (Acts 4:36), but his life demonstrated such an encouraging spirit that the early church leaders gave him the handle of "encourager."

Barnabas is the person who mentored the apostle Paul. Soon after Saul (his name was later changed to Paul) came to Christ, Barnabas took him to the church leadership and defended his claim of salvation (Acts 9:26, 27). "Were it not for Barnabas, who knows what would have happened to Saul—or to the early church? Certainly none of the leaders at Jerusalem wanted anything to do with him."[6]

The story continues in Acts 11:22–26, where again Barnabas strategically influenced the life of this new convert. Note verses 25 and 26: "Then departed Barnabas to Tarsus, for to seek Saul: And when he had found him, he brought him unto Antioch. And it came to pass, that a whole year they assembled themselves with the church, and taught much people."

We find another example of Barnabas' mentoring ministry in the example of young John Mark. This account begins at the end of Acts 12 and continues in Acts 13. Barnabas, still providing a guiding relationship to the emerging leadership of the apostle Paul, was instrumental in taking his relative, John Mark (Col. 4:10), with them on their first missionary journey (Acts 12:25—13:5). You probably know what happened next. John failed. He quit and went back home to Jerusalem. We're not sure exactly why, but that missionary journey didn't go well for this young disciple. Acts 15:38 reveals that a major disagreement broke out between Paul and Barnabas over whether to give John Mark a second chance on the next ministry trip. It is fitting to realize that "Mr. Encouragement" split from Paul and instead took John Mark to Cyprus (Acts 15:39). Barnabas continued his mentoring relationship with this young man even through the difficult times of John Mark's early failure. He did not give up on him.

A major disagreement broke out between Paul and Barnabas.

A subtle yet interesting subplot is interwoven in the fabric of this story of Barnabas and John Mark; we read it in a phrase at the end of Acts 15:39: "Barnabas took Mark, and sailed unto Cyprus." Church history indicates that during that time frame the apostle Peter was probably in Cyprus. Later on, Peter referred to John Mark as his "son," or son in the faith (1 Pet. 5:13).

Peter certainly knew what it meant to fail and then bounce back. He had denied the Lord three times at Christ's crucifixion, and yet he had come back strong to lead the early church. Perhaps it is significant that Barnabas' ministry with young John Mark included taking him to see Peter. John Mark had known Peter from the time Peter had visited his home, the place where the early church met in Acts 12:1–17. I am certain that Peter also had a significant ministry in the life of this young man.

Barnabas did not give up on John Mark.

Note that John Mark did not end up a failure. Sure he struggled; but in the end, even the aged apostle Paul wrote, "Take Mark, and bring him with thee: for he is profitable to me for the ministry" (2 Tim. 4:11).

These three Biblical passages and examples (1 Thessalonians 2, Titus 2, and Barnabas) form the basis of what true mentoring is all about. Mentoring takes work and requires the consistent, self-sacrificing love of an adult who is willing to invest his or her life to encourage and to teach a young person. It demands loving a young person through failures and immaturity and helping him or her mature into a life of service for the Lord.

The Basics of Mentoring

One of the most important things a church can do is to build older people into the lives of its young people, and vice versa. Current postmodern thought often leads to a compartmentalization of life into separate and distinct categories. Churches can impact Millennials (today's high school students) through the consistent and loving interaction of caring adults who take the initiative to be involved in their lives. Although this task may be difficult to accomplish, its rewards are incredibly positive. Through hands-on involvement with adults, teenagers will gain an appreciation for other age groups. *Mentoring happens when adults develop an intentional and proactive personal and growing relationship with individual students to encourage them toward spiritual and personal maturity.*

THE QUALIFICATIONS OF EFFECTIVE MENTORS

Practically speaking, then, what kind of person makes a good mentor? Let me suggest several characteristics.

1. A mentor is an adult who has a strong personal relationship with Jesus Christ and a consistent devotional life.

A mentor has a strong personal relationship with Jesus Christ.

The apostle Paul demonstrated this characteristic with his own personal mentoring ministry. He understood and emphasized mentoring throughout his writings in the Epistles. In passages such as 1 Corinthians 11:1 ("Be ye followers of me, even as I also am of Christ") and 1 Thessalonians 1:6 ("And ye became followers of us and of the Lord"), he taught his followers to imitate him only as he imitated the Lord.

True mentoring begins with adults who possess the characteristics they are attempting to pass along to students. Paul knew that he had to live his personal life the way he wanted his followers to live.

Today's students desperately want to see the reality of a personal, growing relationship with Jesus Christ lived out in the lives of caring adults. Students are not looking for perfection; they understand that perfection is impossible. However, they do want genuineness. They are looking for adults who are real. I am not insinuating that it is okay to excuse sin in some misguided attempt to be real by saying, "Well, that's just the way I am." Students need to see examples of adults who love the Lord and have strong, growing, and victorious relationships with Him.

Of course, the mentor's example must include a consistent devotional life. Again, I refer you to one of the passages that I highlighted earlier. Paul shared two things with his followers in Thessalonica: his own life and the gospel of Christ. Spiritual mentoring today includes those same two priorities. An adult mentor should develop a strong personal relationship with Jesus Christ by spending time in the Word of God, and he or she should make it a priority to demonstrate a testimony before the students.

2. A mentor is an adult who loves teenagers and is willing to spend time with individual kids.

Students are not looking for perfection; they do want genuineness.

Obviously, adult mentors should enjoy spending time with specific teenagers. Yet not all adults have the time or desire to develop personal and growing relationships with students. In fact, "not enough time" is the biggest objection of most adult church members to a mentoring ministry. However, an effective mentoring ministry does not require a specific quantity of time. Mentoring is an adult willing to share his or her life with kids—doing what he or she would normally do, but doing it with individual teenagers. Therefore, good mentors are adults who love students and are willing to share their lives with students.

Once again, we observe this characteristic in Paul's ministry with John Mark and Timothy (Acts 12:25; 16:3). Paul had answered God's call to start churches and to take the gospel to foreign lands; he never wavered from fulfilling that mission. The genius of Paul's mentoring ministry was his willingness to take young men with him as he fulfilled God's calling. Paul's in-

Caring adults encourage students to grow spiritually.

vestment in their lives did not necessarily demand a commitment of extra time on his part. Instead, he taught John Mark and Timothy about ministry by taking them with him on his missionary journeys. Effective mentoring *does* require a commitment of time, but not necessarily a commitment of *extra* time.

3. *A mentor is an adult who has the ability to encourage students to live for the Lord.*

Mentoring is not just spending time with kids. That's not the point. Current news stories are filled with accounts of adults who spend time with kids for negative and harmful purposes. Effective, spiritual mentoring is accomplished by caring adults who encourage students to grow spiritually. Mentors must do everything they can to help their protégés live for the Lord. As the mentor shares his life with students, the students learn how the mentor handles various life situations. Hopefully, as the mentor grows in Christ, the students mature as well.

Mentors need to remember that spiritual growth is a direct result of the work that God's Word does in the lives of God's people. Recall again how Paul exemplified spiritual growth in his life and ministry. As Paul concluded his ministry near the end of his earthly life, he wrote about this truth in his last letter to young Timothy. The familiar passage in 2 Timothy 3:16 and 17 states that God's Word is "profitable" in four specific ways (doctrine, reproof, correction, and instruction in righteousness) for the purpose of spiritual growth in people's lives so that "the man of God may be perfect, throughly furnished unto all good works."

4. A mentor is an adult who is genuine, open, and honest.

Numerous youth ministry organizations have surveyed teenagers to find out what they want in their adult youth leaders. More than any other response, teens want and need youth workers who are real and genuine. Today's students are not looking for spiritual giants. They want mentors who are honest about their own spiritual struggles and their desire to live a victorious Christian life. Students want to see the reality of Jesus Christ lived out in the daily lives of adults.

To make a make a mentoring relationship work, the mentor must demonstrate a consistent walk with the Lord. The apostle Paul willingly shared his life with his student Timothy. In 2 Timothy 3:10 he wrote, "Thou [Timothy] hast fully known my doctrine, manner of life. . . ." He finished that thought a few verses later with these words: "But continue thou in the things which thou hast learned and hast been assured of, knowing of whom thou hast learned them" (v. 14). Timothy could live for the Lord with confidence because he had seen Paul walk with God through many varied and difficult circumstances.

OBJECTIONS TO A MENTORING MINISTRY

You will certainly face some objections from adults as you launch an intentional and organized mentoring ministry. You will face a number of honest but revealing objections. Yet adults and students alike need the practical benefits of a plan to connect the generations.

Howard Hendricks made this observation: "That's one reason I believe so strongly in mentoring. It helps younger men mature and older men rejuvenate. Why? Because we grow most in the process of helping others grow."[7]

Why don't more churches develop a mentoring ministry?

Why is the need for these intergenerational connections largely unmet today? I interviewed a significant number of youth workers and youth pastors and asked them, "Why don't more churches develop a mentoring ministry?" These five objections were mentioned most often.

1. Many adults claim that they are too busy to be mentors.

Undoubtedly, the busyness of today's culture is an obstacle we need to address. People are extremely busy with the demands of their lives and schedules. Again, I must stress that mentoring is not necessarily a commitment of additional time on the part of the adult mentor. Remember that Paul's ministry with John Mark and then Timothy did not require a great amount of extra time. Paul planned to go on his journeys anyway. The young men learned as Paul shared his life and ministry with them.

As you begin a mentoring ministry, be sure to emphasize "Paul's example" with your people, or they will be hesitant to be involved. Examples of this concept are prevalent in our culture through programs like "take your child to work" days, apprenticeships, and internships. Students learn by watching others. This truth stresses the importance for your adult mentors to live consistent spiritual lives. Their students will watch them in action, so to speak, and will learn about living the Christian life from them.

The genius of mentoring is that adults develop an encouraging relationship with students. Building these relationships does not require a great

The genius of mentoring is that it does not require a great deal of extra time.

deal of extra time. As you begin a mentoring ministry, you may want to ask interested adults how much time they can commit to developing a relationship with individual students. Even if they say that they have no extra time to invest in this ministry, they can still be involved in several ways. For instance, an adult can begin mentoring by sitting with a student in church, talking to students in the church foyer, or taking them on errands. The mentor could even take a student to lunch; after all, everyone has to eat. (Chapter 6 includes several ideas for mentoring with various time limits.)

Identify the students who need mentors.

Some willing adults in your church may already have a burden for specific students, and these people may even have a significant amount of time to invest in a mentoring ministry. These mentors can find ways to invest those chunks of time into the lives of student protégés. Opportunities might include playing a round of golf together, making some visits in a local hospital, attending a concert or sporting event together. (Again, I refer you to Chapter 6 for mentoring ideas.)

2. People in both generations may fail to see the practical benefits of mentoring.

You will probably encounter some adults and students who fail to see the benefits of this kind of ministry. Some people are skeptical enough to think that developing these kinds of relationships won't make much difference. That's why you must share positive illustrations and benefits of mentoring. You will recall that I started this book by asking you to remember significant adults who had made an impact on your life when you were young. In Chapter 1 I also gave you some positive Biblical illustrations of mentoring relationships.

I want to emphasize here that I am not interested in talking someone into doing something that he or she does not want to do. Don't worry about the people who are not interested in mentoring. Start with those who are interested. Identify the students who need mentors. Then try to line up interested and caring adults who might fit with those students.

3. Some adults feel inadequate and unprepared to mentor young people.

My guess is that most adults will say that they do not see themselves as qualified to be mentors. Many people have convinced themselves that they don't have what it takes. You will hear excuses such as, "I don't have the training"; "I'm not good with people"; "I can't teach"; or even, "I don't get along very well with teenagers."

Start with those who are interested.

The truth is that younger people almost always look up to and respect older people. Most cultures teach young people to reverence and esteem their elders. In fact, a secular mentoring organization surveyed students all across the country and found that the majority of teenagers want a mentor. Adults may feel inadequate and unprepared, but the vast majority of today's teenagers need and want positive and growing relationships with caring and committed adults.

The majority of teenagers want a mentor.

Again, I quote Howard Hendricks: "But you say, 'I have nothing to offer!' May I challenge that assertion?" Then he elaborates on the potential mentor's experience, knowledge, access, money, resources, friendship or companionship, and time. His conclusion: "If you are in Christ, you always have something to give to other people."[8]

4. People don't know how to mentor.

You may hear people use this objection, but mentoring does not require any one set of skills or abilities. The most effective mentors are those who make themselves available to specific students and demonstrate the reality of Jesus Christ in front of them. We can teach mentors certain techniques of mentoring. Mentors can also learn and hone their people skills through ongoing experiences with others. Later on in this book, I will share with you how effective mentoring can begin and grow into vibrant and committed relationships.

The point is that not knowing how to mentor should not be an excuse. People may not have the ability or skill to teach, preach, or speak publicly. Seek to identify adults who have a genuine and growing relationship with Jesus Christ, love teenagers, and want to encourage them to live for the Lord. Those people make good mentors. As Proverbs 13:20 states, "He that walketh with wise men shall be wise." That statement is an apt description of mentoring.

5. Some people will say that no one ever asked them to mentor anyone.

Do you remember the famous "I Want You for the U.S. Army" recruiting poster? It featured Uncle Sam with his long, bony finger pointed straight at the viewer. That marketing campaign met with great success. It was pointed and personal. And it was effective. No one could escape it.

Why not use the same basic campaign to recruit people as mentors? Use slogans such as, "If you are a student, you need a mentor," or "If you are an adult, you should be a mentor."

Students need the godly example of older Christians.

What a shame that the modern church has moved away from the New Testament model of connecting the generations (Titus 2:1–10). Many churches totally separate the youth group from the overall life of the church. This separation is a big mistake. Students need the godly example of older Christians, and older people need the energy and life of young people.

The teenagers in your church may never verbally say, "I want a mentor." But I believe with all my heart that they do want—and need—mentors. Consider polling the teens in your church to gain their opinions on mentoring. I think you will find the majority of them are open to it and willing to develop a relationship with adult mentors. So in a sense they *are* asking for mentors. And beside that, God is asking for mentors.

Let's pray that God will use each of us to recruit, motivate, and instruct adult mentors to initiate personal, growing relationships in the lives of students in our churches.

CHAPTER 3

Recruiting Effective Mentors

The focus of this book is how to begin and then implement a successful and practical mentoring ministry in your church. The "fit" between the adult mentor and the student recipient is one of the key elements of any mentoring relationship

OPTIONS FOR MAKING THE
MENTOR/STUDENT CONNECTION

I will discuss three basic means of selecting which students fit specific adult mentors by listing some pros and cons of each approach. It is not my intention to determine the best selection process for your church. Extenuating circumstances may make one of the methods more suitable for your specific situation. The goal for each church is to begin making intentional intergenerational connections. Teenagers need mentors, and adults need to share their lives, their experiences, and their knowledge with students. My advice is to think through the following ideas and prayerfully consider the best approach for your ministry.

1. Adults select students.

Barnabas intentionally sought out Saul, or Paul.

Certainly it makes sense to ask the adults to select the students they feel comfortable mentoring. The potential mentor could select teens with similar interests and from similar backgrounds.

Two Biblical illustrations indicate that this approach is somewhat practical. Barnabas intentionally sought out Saul, or Paul (Acts 9:27); and Paul intentionally recruited Timothy to accompany him on his journey (Acts 16:1–3).

The major weakness that I see in this method of selection is the likelihood that the neediest students might not be included. Humanly speaking, it is natural for adults to select athletes and/or musicians. They may not select a physically challenged kid or a student with emotional needs. Perhaps I'm wrong in thinking this way, but I have found that our fleshly nature leads us to make natural connections with popular, outgoing kids instead of those who need a mentor the most.

2. Students select mentors.

The second option for making mentor-to-protégé connections is to allow each student to select an adult mentor. Again, this idea has its own merits. The student may look for an adult who seems to have what he or she needs. Or the teens may identify adults who have shown an interest in them and their activities. For example, a high school athlete could look for an adult mentor who is interested in sports and willing to go to games with him. The same idea is true with music, drama, auto mechanics, computers—almost anything.

Again, I see some weaknesses to this approach. Let me ask you a couple of pointed questions. What if the adult rebuffs the student? What if a needy student is not confident enough to approach an adult? These things should be carefully considered before implementing a mentoring ministry.

3. Someone in leadership makes the selection.

The third option is for someone in leadership at the church to make the connection between adult mentors and student protégés. Perhaps the pastor, a youth pastor, a youth worker, or some other church leader possesses the most objectivity in making sound selections. This person needs to be someone who knows each student and has a basic knowledge of the students' needs and interests. This leader must determine which students need mentors and arrange the initial meetings between those

fit potentional mentors with needy students who have similar backgrounds and interests.

students and caring, available adults. He or she could fit potential mentors with needy students who have similar backgrounds and interests.

I have found it very difficult for anyone other than a youth group leader or someone very familiar with the youth ministry to arrange a mentoring relationship. The church leadership may have good intentions and may be objective, but human connections do not necessarily work that way. It's easy to make person-to-person relationships look good on paper, but in real life a human spark of interest, a connection, and a rapport must be present. And, of course, both the mentor and the student must have a desire to make the relationship work. These things are never a certainty on paper. They are qualities that must be worked out in real-life situations.

don't be too concerned if a specific mentoring relationship fails.

Each method of selection offers strengths and weaknesses. If the Lord has put a burden on your heart to develop an intentional mentoring ministry in your church, you should pray faithfully about how to make the specific personal connections. Perhaps a little trial and error is acceptable. After all, the development of any human relationship is never an exact science. But the reality is that the Lord must direct this entire process. Never look at mentoring as something you can administrate and then walk away from. You don't want your students to feel like they are guinea pigs in a scientist's laboratory. You want them to know that several adults in your church care about students and would love to have a hands-on, mentoring relationship with them. Students need intergenerational connections. Mentoring is an intentional way for that to happen.

Don't be too concerned if a specific mentoring relationship fails. Work to make another connection happen. Even if one mentoring relationship fails, at least the two generations have made a connection with each other and have gotten to know other people better. After all, even the Biblical account of Barnabas' mentoring relationship with Paul is a story of a strained relationship (Acts 15:37–40). Yet the end result was that both men developed other connections and continued on for the Lord.

FITTING ADULT MENTORS WITH SPECIFIC STUDENTS

As you endeavor to start this type of ministry, keep in mind the principles listed in this section.

1. Pray that the Lord will give adults a burden for specific teens.

Pray specifically for individual teens.

Obviously, prayer is the place to start. As you encourage the adults in your church to consider a mentoring ministry, ask them to pray specifically for individual teens. You may be able to facilitate this process by distributing a prayer list of the teenagers in your youth group. As the adults begin to pray, the Lord will give them a burden for specific kids. The method you choose for encouraging people to pray is flexible. You may want to call a special prayer meeting or encourage more individualized prayer instead. Be sure not to ignore this important first step. This ministry must be bathed in prayer. You want God's blessing and God's fit between mentor and student.

Start your mentoring emphasis with the neediest students.

2. *Identify teens with specific needs and those who need encouragement.*

Undoubtedly, your church has many teenagers who, for whatever reason, need special encouragement from godly and caring adults. These students may be loners or have obvious family needs (e.g., single-parent homes, absentee parents, recent death in the family). Ask the adults in your church to consider giving these kids some mentoring attention. In other words, start your mentoring emphasis with the neediest students. Most likely, the popular kids in your church (e.g., the gifted and talented musicians and athletes) are getting a great deal of attention from adults already. The point is, be careful not to ignore the students who need mentors the most.

3. *Adults should consider mentoring students with similar interests.*

A natural tie may exist between certain adults and

students in your church because of their similar interests in cars or auto mechanics, computers, golfing, hunting, crafts, shopping, sports, visiting the library, gardening, or countless other things. You will be amazed at how adults will have interests that relate to today's teenagers. Likewise, the teens may possess skills or expertise in various areas that could benefit the adults. For instance, many teenagers have incredible computer skills that they might be willing to teach to unskilled adults.

4. *Parents of teenagers should think about developing a mentoring relationship with some of their kids' friends.*

Encourage parents to develop positive relationships with some of their own children's friends, especially students from broken homes or dysfunctional families. These natural ties present great openings for adults to impact needy kids. The parents should look for practical opportunities to make initial contacts with these teens; e.g., invite needy teens to their home to visit their kids.

The key to this chapter is that students need mentors. Don't be overly worried about developing a perfect fit. God can certainly work that out. It is a natural human reaction to develop relationships with people who have similar interests or experiences. Any amount of encouragement that an adult can give to a student will be helpful and beneficial.

Students need mentors.

CHAPTER 4

Now What?

Once the adults identify their potential protégés, they need to begin developing a personal and growing relationship with that person or persons. The investment of time will certainly vary, depending upon each adult and student. Often mentoring relationships start slowly and then develop into deeper interaction. For the most part, the adults should focus on being faithful and consistent.

Remember, good relationships take time. Share the following observations with your adult mentors to help them get started in their mentoring relationships.

✓ Encourage the mentors to pray for positive connections with the students and for God to prepare the hearts of the students for a mentoring relationship.

✓ Ask the mentors to make initial contacts with the students. The adults should make the first informal contact, possibly before or after a church service.

An informal meeting at church takes any threat out of the contact between the adults and students. In addition, the students will see this program as an opportunity that the church has arranged to connect people from various generations.

✓ The first meeting between mentors and students should also take place in a nonthreatening, informal public place. The adults should be sensitive to the students' wishes in this matter. Encourage the adults to keep the conversation light and casual. They need to develop relationships with students, and it will definitely take more than one meeting to build those relationships.

✓ Persuade mentors to begin their relationships by sharing something about themselves. They could include a brief salvation testimony and a little bit about their backgrounds or interests. Once the adults have shared, the teens will more likely open up and discuss spiritual things. The key to the initial meeting is just to get to know one another. Tell the adults not to force anything. Students can share more personal or sensitive information later when the relationship has progressed. Mentors can ask students about their salvation, family, background, interests or hobbies, and goals and dreams. Advise adults to start with low-risk discussion matters and then move to more in-depth, personal matters later.

Good relationships take time.

✓ At subsequent meetings, instruct the mentors to ask the students for their testimonies. Encourage the mentors to look for openings to talk about salvation, but caution them about putting the students on the defensive.

✓ The mentors should plan times when they can get together with their students. Each person involved will need to be flexible and creative. Certainly today's adults have busy schedules, but so do the teens. Coordinating schedules may prove to be one of the most difficult parts of the entire mentoring process. Encourage people to go over their calendars together and to work out suitable times to meet. (We will talk more about this issue later. I will give you some specific ideas that can work even in very busy schedules.) In the beginning, the contacts may be of a more superficial nature, such as sending postcards or e-mails or Instant Messages. Other possibilities include sitting together in a church service or talking in the hallway. Future meetings could then take place at fast-food restaurants or at the adult's home.

Ask students for their testimonies.

✓ Stress that the mentors should pray for their protégés by name every day. You may also want to encourage the students to pray for their mentors. I am always amazed at how God uses prayer to develop a growing concern for the people I am praying for. I found this to be true with missionaries I don't even know. As I pray for the people on my church's missionary list, I have found that God puts such a burden on my heart for them that by the time the missionaries return home on furlough, I feel like I know them personally because I have been praying specifically for them and their needs.

Encourage students to walk with God.

✓ Mentors should encourage the students to walk with God. Mentoring is a process to help the teens grow spiritually. True mentoring is not *just* hanging out with teenagers. Mentoring is the process of investing in the life of a student. It is a caring adult demonstrating what it means to live for the Lord. Mentors should do everything they can to encourage the teens spiritually without being preachy, controlling, or negative.

✓ Encourage the mentors to offer help to the students. Students might need help with their homework or school projects. They might need mechanical help with their car, a ride to work, or other practical assistance. Offering to help the student is a specific way in which the mentor can build a positive relationship with a teenager and his or her family.

Let's pray that God will use each of us to recruit, motivate, and train adult mentors to have personal, growing relationships in the lives of students.

Making Mentoring Practical

Okay, you know that mentoring is important. You understand that today's students need the godly influence of adults in their lives. You know that the intergenerational approach to youth ministry is effective. I have listed ways to make mentoring work and ways to fit adult mentors with students in your youth group. You have also read several ways to get this kind of ministry started.

Now I want to be honest: you should think through the following guidelines and cautions before you implement a mentoring ministry in your church.

GUIDELINES

1. Mentors should always be sensitive to the needs and concerns of the students' parents.

Because I am suggesting that adults build relationships with teenagers, can you understand that this idea has the potential to make some parents and church leaders extremely nervous?

The church should take the initiative by communicating with the parents how the mentoring ministry

nurture a positive rapport with the teens' parents.

will work. Be sure to instruct the adult mentors to be open and sensitive to the concerns of the teens' parents. The mentoring process should start slowly and should build into a relationship over time. Adult mentors should also work hard to nurture a positive rapport with the teens' parents. Also, encourage the mentors not to be critical of the teens' parents or attempt to serve as their parents. The mentor's responsibility is to support the parents and promote the parents' role to the student.

If a teen's parents are uncomfortable or uncertain about this relationship, I have found that it is best for the mentor to back off until the parents are supportive of the mentoring arrangement.

2. Mentors should build relationships with those of the same gender.

This guideline should be obvious, but we need to emphasize it. In today's culture many predators and abuse situations readily exist. That's why men should build relationships with young men and women with young women. Remember that Scripture encourages this guideline (e.g., Titus 2, Paul's relationship with John Mark and Timothy, and even in Christ's relationship with His disciples). Even so, adults must be careful to have proper motives and to be blameless in this process. Again, start slowly and build the relationships over time.

3. Mentors should seek to develop positive relationships with the students, not try to control them.

I've observed that many adults try to point out faults in the lives of the students and control the relationship. We must guard against this practice. As the mentoring relationship grows, the adult may be able to point out weaknesses and needs in the life of the student, but please warn your adults not to start the mentoring relationship that way. The mentors should be kind and respectful. They need to encourage, not discourage their young protégés.

4. Mentors should stay in communication with the church leadership.

One of the fallouts of this ministry may be that these caring, open adults will discover things about the teenagers that are of a personal nature. As the mentors develop growing, encouraging, personal relationships with the teenagers, they are likely to learn shocking—even quite dangerous—things about some

Mentors need to encourage, not discourage.

teenagers. Mentors need the emotional and spiritual maturity to handle this knowledge in a Biblical manner. They also need to learn the balance of keeping confidential things to themselves and knowing when to share things that might be sinful or dangerous to the teen. This reason shows the importance of the church in initiating the mentoring ministry. The church leadership needs to be involved in this process and should have some input as to which adults serve as mentors.

Mentors must guard their own family lives.

5. *Mentors must guard their own family lives and their personal walk with the Lord.*

As these mentoring relationships develop, it would be easy for the mentors to spend more and more time with the student at the expense of the mentor's family or personal walk with God. It is critically important for adult mentors to establish and continue a strong, consistent devotional life by spending quality time each day in God's Word. It is also very important for the adult to make sure that his or her own family life is on solid ground. In fact, one of the best things that any adult can demonstrate to teenagers is a strong, growing, and loving family life. Many of today's kids rarely see the model of a strong marriage and family.

CAUTION

We should consider one extremely important caution when we discuss adults interacting with students. That's the matter of trust and safety—or actually, child abuse. Let's face it: there are predators out there. It's tragic but nevertheless true in today's culture. News reports contain many instances of physical and sexual abuse between adults and minors. We pray that abuse does not happen, but we also must take precautions to keep bad situations from occurring. Churches should do everything they can to protect the juveniles who are entrusted to them.

I strongly advise youth workers to obtain trusted legal advice on this subject and then to implement key safeguards into the fabric of their ministries. Some of these safeguards could include asking potential adult mentors to fill out brief written applications stating why they want to be mentors. In some cases it may be worthwhile to consider using a professional investigative organization, such as the local sheriff's office, to conduct background checks. This process indicates why it is so important to consult with legal authorities about what information is needed for adult volunteers to work with youth in your church.

Take precautions to keep bad situations from occurring.

We shouldn't overreact here, however. Our goal is to

involve significant, trusted adults in the lives of students. We want to recruit mentors, not turn people away from serving in this capacity. The important thing is to bathe this entire process in prayer. Ask the Lord for His wisdom. He can direct and guide. He also can close the door to keep negative and harmful relationships from developing.

Involve significant, trusted adults in the lives of students.

I strongly recommend that all youth workers read Jack Crabtree's book *Better Safe Than Sued,* published by Group Books (available from Regular Baptist Press). It contains helpful advice on keeping out of trouble in youth ministry.

CHAPTER 6

Ideas for Mentoring Connections

The key to any mentoring relationship is the ability of the adult to make significant, personal connections with his or her student protégé. I do want to give credit to whom credit is due. I have seen the following mentoring connection ideas in various sources. However, I obtained most of the ideas from *Purpose-Driven Youth Ministry* by Doug Fields[9] and from *The Student Mentoring Handbook,* developed by Bryan and Sheri Waggoner, Bill Newman, and Lori Watkins.[10]

Take a few minutes to study this list. It illustrates that even very busy people can get involved in the mentoring process.

MENTORING CONNECTIONS

**If adults say, "I have no extra time to invest,"
encourage them to**

- sit with students in youth group, Sunday School, or church;
- take youth on errands;
- ask students to help with a project;
- invite youth to their homes for a meal;
- meet students at a restaurant (you have to eat anyway);
- greet youth with a big smile, handshake, or pat on the back;
- ask for a prayer request and then pray on the spot;
- give students something (book, CD);
- share a blessing or prayer request;
- take youth to work with them;
- sponsor teens for a youth group activity or missions trip.

**If the adults say, "I have fifteen minutes a week,"
they could**

- write a note of encouragement;
- send an e-mail or Instant Message;
- make a phone call;
- drive teens home from youth group, church, or an activity;
- initiate one-on-one conversations before or after meetings;
- brag on the students to their parents;
- pray for a specific need each day;
- compliment teens in front of someone else.

If the adults say, "I have thirty minutes a week,"
they could
   • go to thirty minutes of an event (sports, drama,
     music, youth group);
   • meet for accountability or prayer;
   • drop in on youth at work (if appropriate);
   • pray for specific needs each day;
   • provide transportation to and from an activity or
     work.

If the adults say, "I have two hours a week," they
could
   • visit in the students' homes;
   • invite youth to an evening in their homes;
   • go out to eat with students;
   • take parents out to dinner;
   • help with homework;
   • do a service project or craft together;
   • pop a bag of popcorn and hang out;
   • go shopping together;
   • wash and wax car;
   • listen to CDs together;
   • involve youth in a hobby of yours;
   • discuss devotions together;
   • discuss a spiritual question;
   • go on an activity together (e.g., miniature golfing,
     bowling);
   • do a Bible study;
   • go on visitation;
   • take a gift to a needy friend.

If the adults say, "I have four hours a week," they could
- play a round of golf;
- go on a hike;
- attend a ball game;
- make a video;
- volunteer at a mission;
- read/discuss a Bible study book;
- teach youth a new skill;
- attend a Christian concert;
- work together at church.

If the adults say, "I have ten hours a week," they could
- go on a campout;
- clean/organize something;
- paint or build something;
- organize a food drive and deliver to a needy family;
- start a new ministry.

CHAPTER 7

What about Parents Mentoring Their Own Kids?

Let's talk about one more specific question concerning the mentoring concept: What about parents mentoring their kids?

Obviously, that would be a good idea, but let's face reality: many parents do not have the time or do not take the time to get actively involved in the lives of their own kids. I have a theory about many of today's Baby Boomer parents. This generation of parents (of whom I am a member) tends to talk a lot about "the family," but these parents do very little with their families. That is to our shame.

Let me give you a rather current illustration of my point. The suicide plane crashes at New York's World

Trade Center happened on September 11, 2001, around
8:45 A.M., but many of the people who worked in those
complexes were not at their offices yet. We live in an up-
wardly mobile society, and it is nothing for people who
live near large cities to commute to and from work many
hours each day. That is why many of the employees in

Work and careers dominate the lives of today's Baby Boomer parents.

those buildings had not yet
arrived at work when those
disasters happened. (Praise
the Lord!) Work and careers
dominate the lives of to-
day's Baby Boomer parents.
Yes, they tend to talk much
about how important their
families are to them. But
when we look at their
lifestyles, we note that they
often ignore their families, or, at best, slight them in fa-
vor of other priorities. Many of today's parents choose to
buy things for their families rather than spend time with
them. Money they have; it's time they are struggling
with.

So how can we, as local church youth workers, encourage the parents in our churches to actually spend
the time it takes to mentor their own children? Let me
remind you of the definition of mentoring that I used
previously. *Mentoring is an adult taking the initiative to
develop a personal, growing relationship with individual
students to encourage spiritual and personal maturity.*
Here, then, are some specific, practical suggestions to
encourage parents:

1. Publicly present the idea of mentoring to your church.

During such a presentation, mention that parents can intentionally develop this kind of relationship with their own kids. I have found that the Lord uses His Word to develop a burden in the hearts and lives of people for ministry. Perhaps, therefore, the Lord will give you the opportunity to preach or teach on the subject of mentoring. If you do not have pulpit exposure in your church, you may want to discuss this concept with the senior pastor or pastoral staff as one step toward getting them to "buy in" to this important avenue of ministry. Or try to schedule and publicize a meeting for all who are interested. Be sure to emphasize during each step along the way that parents can indeed have this kind of relationship with their own teenagers.

2. Show parents some practical ways to develop mentoring relationships with their kids.

One way to do that is to reproduce the list of "Mentoring Connections" in Chapter 6. Your people are extremely busy. Parents have many time commitments already. That's why we need to show them that they can develop solid, hands-on mentoring relationships with small amounts of time. For instance, they eat three times a day. Why not take their son or daughter out for lunch? They may travel for business.

Parents can have this kind of relationship with their own teenagers.

Why not take one of their children with them on a business trip? They probably have time to write short e-mails or make quick phone calls to their kids. Certainly parents can (and should) pray specifically for their children and plan times in their schedules for parents and teens to pray together. The truth is, we probably all have the time. It is a matter of how we use our time.

It is a matter of how we use our time.

3. Provide resources to equip and train parents who want to mentor their children.

In the past several years, my wife and I have had the privilege of speaking in parenting conferences for parents of teenagers and preteens. It is a real joy to help and encourage parents as they seek to raise their teenagers in the "nurture and admonition of the Lord." Your church could host such a seminar, or you could provide parents with practical and helpful books on the subject of parenting teenagers. Here is a list of books that I have found helpful to parents of teenagers:

She Said Yes: The Unlikely Martyrdom of Cassie Bernall by Misty Bernall, published by W Publishing Group.

The Seven Checkpoints: Seven Principles Every Teenager Needs to Know by Andy Stanley and Stuart Hall, published by Howard Publishing.

Age of Opportunity: A Biblical Guide to Parenting Teens by Paul David Tripp, published by P & R Publishing.

Shepherding a Child's Heart by Tedd Tripp, published by Shepherd Press.

The Pro-Teen Parent: The 10 Best Ways to Cheer on Your Teen's Growth in God by Daniel Hahn, published by Multnomah Publishers.

But, You Don't Understand: How to Know That You're Doing the Right Thing with Your Kids by Paul Borthwick, published by Thomas Nelson (out of print).

Escaping the Subtle Sellout: Family Strategies for Living in a World of Compromise by Dewey Bertolini, published by Victor Books.

Family-Based Youth Ministry by Mark DeVries, published by InterVarsity Press.

Bringing Your Teen Back to God by Robert Laurent, published by David C. Cook.

Please understand that Regular Baptist Press DOES NOT necessarily endorse the doctrinal positions of these authors or publishers. These books are listed because they may be of help to parents of teenagers. I highly encourage pastors and youth workers to read these books with discernment before they recommend them to anyone else.

Schedule a parent/teen fellowship.

4. Organize ways for parents to interact with their own teenagers.

Your local church provides ways for people of the same basic age group to get together for mutual encouragement, training, and fellowship. Why not schedule a parent/teen fellowship for your church? Some churches put on nice banquets, while others organize picnics or other functions. The teenagers and youth workers in my church host a "parent appreciation banquet" for the parents of teenagers each year. Each of our church's youth workers takes part in the program. They present the year's youth ministry schedule and communicate other important items. The kids and their parents really enjoy this well-organized event.

When I was a youth pastor, I taught a Sunday School class from time to time for the parents of teenagers in our church. I shared Biblical principles of parenting and talked about what was going on in the contemporary youth culture. We used that time to keep parents up-to-date on the youth ministry, and it gave them an opportunity to get to know the other parents of teenagers in our church.

Hopefully these ideas will help you teach parents to mentor their own kids.

Conclusion

GODLY AND CARING adults can indeed have a significant and encouraging ministry in the lives of today's students. As a reminder, mentoring doesn't necessarily mean a commitment of extra time on the part of adults; instead, mentoring is doing what you would normally do, but doing it with a teenager (or two). Adult mentors must be willing to share their lives with their protégés to encourage them to walk with the Lord and to go on for Him. Mentoring does not replace church services, Sunday School lessons, Bible studies, or youth group meetings. Mentoring goes on all around those things. It happens in church hallways, in restaurants, in office buildings, and in the homes of adults. Mentoring is real life, and it must be done in real-life situations.

Several years ago, I came across the following poem that aptly describes the ministry of mentoring. I trust it will be an encouragement to you as you consider the development of an intentional mentoring ministry in your church.

I'd Rather See a Sermon

I'd rather see a sermon than hear one
    any day;
I'd rather one should walk with me
    than merely tell the way.
The eye's a better pupil and more will-
    ing than the ear,
Fine counsel is confusing, but
    example's always clear;
And the best of all the preachers are the
    men who live their creeds,
For to see good put in action is what
    everybody needs.
I soon can learn to do it if you'll let me
    see it done;
I can watch your hands in action, but
    your tongue too fast may run.
And the lecture you deliver may be
    very wise and true,
But I'd rather get my lessons by observ-
    ing what you do;
For I might misunderstand you and the
    high [advice] you give
But there's no misunderstanding how
    you act and how you live.[11]

Notes

1. Timothy Smith, *The Seven Cries of Today's Teens* (Brentwood, Tenn.: Integrity Publishers, 2003), 5.

2. Homer, *The Odyssey,* trans. E. V. Rieu (New York: Penguin Books, 1946), 50.

3. The Harvard Mentoring Project, www.whomentoredyou.org

4. Howard G. Hendricks and William D. Hendricks, *As Iron Sharpens Iron: Building Character in a Mentoring Relationship* (Chicago: Moody Press, 1995), 232.

5. Kenneth S. Wuest, *Wuest's Word Studies: The Pastoral Studies in the Greek New Testament for the English Reader* (Grand Rapids: Wm. B. Eerdmans Publishing Co., 1952), 191.

6. Hendricks, 130.

7. Hendricks, 149.

8. Hendricks, 136–138.

9. Doug Fields, *Purpose-Driven Youth Ministry* (Grand Rapids: Zondervan Publishing House, 1998), 300.

10. Bryan Waggoner, et al., *The Student Mentoring Handbook* (Brownsburg, Ind.: Youth Alive Student Ministries, 2001), 10, 11.

11. *Collected Verse of Edgar A. Guest* (Chicago: Contemporary Books, Inc., 1934), 599.

Selected Bibliography

Biehl, Bobb. *Mentoring: Confidence in Finding a Mentor and Becoming One.* Nashville: Broadman & Holman Publishers, 1996.

Briscoe, Jill, Laurie Katz McIntyre, and Beth Seversen. *Designing Effective Women's Ministries.* Grand Rapids: Zondervan Publishing House, 1995.

Engstrom, Ted W. *The Fine Art of Mentoring: Passing On to Others What God Has Given to You.* Newburgh, Ind.: Trinity Press, 1989.

Fields, Doug. *Purpose-Driven Youth Ministry.* Grand Rapids: Zondervan Publishing House, 1998.

Hendricks, Howard G., and William D. Hendricks. *As Iron Sharpens Iron: Building Character in a Mentoring Relationship.* Chicago: Moody Press, 1995.

Homer. *The Odyssey.* Translated by E. V. Rieu. New York: Penguin Books, 1946.

Smith, Timothy. *The Seven Cries of Today's*
Brentwood, Tenn.: Integrity Publishers, 2003.

Swindoll, Charles R. *Paul: A Man of Grace and Grit.*
Nashville: The W Publishing Group, 2002.

Waggoner, Bryan, Sheri Waggoner, Bill Newman,
and Lori Watkins. *The Student Mentoring Handbook.* Brownsburg, Ind.: Youth Alive Student
Ministries, 2001.

Wuest, Kenneth S. *Wuest's Word Studies: The Pastoral
Studies in the Greek New Testament for the English
Reader.* Grand Rapids: Wm. B. Eerdmans Publish-
ing Co., 1952.